Instant RaphaelJS Starter

Get to grips with RaphaelJS - a powerful cross-browser compatible vector graphics library, to create interactive 2D graphics and animations with ease

A.Krishna sagar

PUBLISHING

BIRMINGHAM - MUMBAI

Instant RaphaelJS Starter

First published: January 2013

Production Reference: 1180113

Published by Packt Publishing Ltd.
Livery Place
35 Livery Street
Birmingham B3 2PB, UK.

ISBN 978-1-78216-985-7

www.packtpub.com

Credits

Author

A.Krishna sagar

Reviewer

Flarnie Marchán

Acquisition Editor

Mary Nadar

Commissioning Editor

Ameya Sawant

Technical Editors

Charmaine Pereira

Sadhana Varma

Copy Editor

Insiya Morbiwala

Project Coordinator

Sherin Padayatty

Proofreader

Maria Gould

Graphics

Aditi Gajjar

Production Coordinator

Prachali Bhiwandkar

Cover Work

Prachali Bhiwandkar

Cover Image

Conidon Miranda

About the Author

A.Krishna sagar is a professional web developer and designer who has a love for creativity and enjoys experimenting with various frontend web technologies. He is a technical enthusiast specializing in frontend development (JavaScript, jQuery, CSS3, HTML5, Canvas, RaphaelJS, WebGL, and Google Maps JavaScript API), with over 4 years of industrial experience.

As a techie, he has a clear logical and analytical thought process for solving problems, and has a deep understanding of what he does. Apart from being good at what he does, he is also an excellent learner who always dives into new web technologies and accepts challenges willingly.

As a person, he is an optimistic, fun loving, and out of the box thinker. Though he did his Bachelor's degree in Biotechnology, his enthusiasm for Internet technologies led him to do an NIIT course in Computer Science at the same time, and he later acquired an MSc degree in Computer Science.

I would like to express my gratitude to the many people who saw me through this book—to all those who provided their support, talked things over, read, wrote, offered comments, allowed me to quote their remarks, and assisted in editing, proofreading, and designing.

I would especially like to thank my family and friends for their support.

About the Reviewer

Flarnie Marchán is a professional freelancer specializing in web design and frontend development (JavaScript, HTML, and CSS). She shares her passion for design and technology at `flarnie.com/blog`. Be sure to check it out, or get in touch at `flarnie.com/contact`.

www.packtpub.com

Support files, eBooks, discount offers and more

You might want to visit www.PacktPub.com for support files and downloads related to your book.

Did you know that Packt offers eBook versions of every book published, with PDF and ePub files available? You can upgrade to the eBook version at www.PacktPub.com and as a print book customer, you are entitled to a discount on the eBook copy. Get in touch with us at service@packtpub.com for more details.

At www.PacktPub.com, you can also read a collection of free technical articles, sign up for a range of free newsletters and receive exclusive discounts and offers on Packt books and eBooks.

packtLib.packtpub.com

Do you need instant solutions to your IT questions? PacktLib is Packt's online digital book library. Here, you can access, read and search across Packt's entire library of books.

Why Subscribe?

- ✦ Fully searchable across every book published by Packt
- ✦ Copy and paste, print and bookmark content
- ✦ On demand and accessible via web browser

Free Access for Packt account holders

If you have an account with Packt at www.PacktPub.com, you can use this to access PacktLib today and view nine entirely free books. Simply use your login credentials for immediate access.

Table of Contents

Instant RaphaelJS Starter

Welcome to *Instant RaphaelJS Starter*.

This book has especially been created to provide you with all the information that you need to set up RaphaelJS. You will learn the basics of RaphaelJS, get started with building your first script, and discover some tips and tricks for using RaphaelJS.

This document contains the following sections:

So what is RaphaelJS? – Find out what RaphaelJS actually is, what you can do with it, and why it's so great.

Installation – Learn how to download and install RaphaelJS with minimum fuss and then set it up so that you can use it as soon as possible.

Quick start – This section will show you how to perform one of the core tasks of RaphaelJS, that is, creating shapes. Follow the steps to create your own shape, which will be the basis of most of your work in RaphaelJS.

Top features you need to know about – Here you will learn how to perform five tasks with the most important features of RaphaelJS.

People and places you should get to know – Every open source project is centered around a community. This section provides you with many useful links to the project page and forums, as well as a number of helpful articles, tutorials, blogs, and the Twitter feeds of RaphaelJS super contributors.

So, what is RaphaelJS?

RaphaelJS is a vector graphics library, which is used to draw objects in the browser.

In this section, we will see what RaphaelJS is, how it is different from other similar drawing libraries, and how it sets itself apart from **HTML5 Canvas**.

Two-headed and three-lettered

Almost a decade ago, we had a great technology called **Scalable Vector Graphics** (**SVG**), which was derived from **Vector Markup Language** (**VML**) to draw simple to complex 2D graphics on browsers. SVG was a **World Wide Web Consortium** (**W3C**) specification and was there lingering in the minds of advanced developers for a decade or so. VML, on the other hand, was Microsoft's specification and existed even before SVG. Though SVG was inspired from VML, they were never fond of each other and never co-existed on the same browser. SVG ran on all browsers except Internet Explorer (IE 9 and above supports SVG) and vice versa.

A two-headed and three-lettered headache.

The marriage of two problems and the birth of RaphaelJS

SVG was a beautiful baby but no one wanted the labor pains—coding using SVG and VML for cross-browser consistency was so much of a serious pain that most developers simply used images. So we had two different technologies, both doing the same thing but they were both significantly different in their syntaxes and never ran on the same browser. It seemed like there was a problem in getting them to peacefully co-exist.

JavaScript – the binder of oddities

JavaScript bound these two giants together and out of their marriage was born RaphaelJS, inheriting the best charms of both parents. It has the ability to scale almost any browser's turf and dance to any developer's tune.

The solution—RaphaelJS.

Browser support

Most browsers support SVG and all versions of IE from IE 5.0 onwards support VML. Since RaphaelJS was developed to make the most of SVG and VML, it can practically run in almost any browser, making it more reliable.

RaphaelJS—the amphibian

What is RaphaelJS and what is not RaphaelJS?

We now know what RaphaelJS is—it's a combination of SVG and VML using whichever of these two technologies the current browser supports, therefore it is versatile and reliable. But it's equally important to also know what is not RaphaelJS.

A little about vector and raster graphics

Just like the world is of two primary states water and land, graphics are of two primitive types—vector and raster. Vector graphics are drawn using geometrical primitives like lines, curves, ellipses, and so on. Various such primitives join together and form a graphic. Vector graphics are drawn on the screen mathematically. They are scalable without loss in quality. Raster graphics, on the other hand, are pixel-based and are not scalable. The main advantage with vector graphics is that they are scalable and are also real objects, meaning we can fiddle with them and manipulate them dynamically. The following diagram shows the difference between raster (bitmap) and vector graphics:

Difference between raster (bitmap) and vector graphics

RaphaelJS as a vector

RaphaelJS is a vector graphics library, therefore the drawings are real DOM objects. Thus they can be dynamically accessed, manipulated, resized, and practically hammered into anything you want in runtime. Best of all is that they can be assigned events like `click`, `mouseover`, `mouseleave`, and so on. The capabilities of RaphaelJS are just incredible.

Raphael uses vector graphics and HTML 5 Canvas uses raster graphics.

The x, y positioning that RaphaelJS uses

RaphaelJS uses the x, y positioning system to draw. The top-left corner of the screen is 0,0 and the horizontal scale is the x axis and the vertical scale is the y axis.

So if the code says (15,20) then it means that the point will be at 15 points from the x axis (horizontal) and 20 points from the y axis (vertical).

RaphaelJS is a vector graphics-based library built to make it easier to draw on the screen. RaphaelJS uses either SVG or VML, whichever the current browser supports. The drawings created using RaphaelJS are DOM objects and can be manipulated dynamically making them more versatile, they can also be assigned events such as `click`, `mouseover`, and `mouseleave`. All these amazing properties make RaphaelJS exciting to learn and use.

 RaphaelJS and HTML 5 Canvas are two different things entirely. Though they both appear to do similar things (drawing), they are different in how they do it. RaphaelJS is based on vector graphics and HTML5 Canvas is raster-based.

Installation

Installing and setting up RaphaelJS is very simple, it's as simple as downloading the latest RaphaelJS file and including it in HTML.

In three easy steps, you can install RaphaelJS and get it set up.

Step 1 – What do I need?

Before you install RaphaelJS, you will need to check that you have all of the following required elements:

+ A web browser
+ A text editor

Step 2 – Downloading RaphaelJS

The easiest way to download RaphaelJS is as a minified JS, from `https://raw.github.com/DmitryBaranovskiy/raphael/master/raphael-min.js`.

RaphaelJS, unlike most libraries, does not have any other dependencies, so it's just `raphael.js`.

Since RaphaelJS is a JavaScript plugin, the download link will show a plain JavaScript file in the browser. You should copy the text and paste it into a new file named `raphael.js` (or any name you prefer), and save it to your JavaScript directory or to any location in your server.

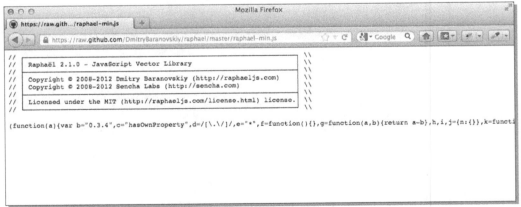

Minified RaphaelJS code shown in the browser

Step 3 – Adding it to the HTML

Include it in the bottom section of your HTML page using the `<script>` tag and point the `src` attribute to the path where the `raphael.js` file is located.

```
<!DOCTYPE html>
<html>
    <head>
        <title>Raphael JS</title>
    </head>
    <body>
        <div id="canvas" style="width:140px;padding:0px;margin:0px;"></div>
        <!--Some HTML content-->

        <!--Script at the bottom of the page-->
        <script type="text/javascript" src="raphael.js" /></script>
    </body>
</html>
```

Script included at the bottom

The browser reads the HTML code in a linear fashion. If there is a script tag at the top, the browser will download the script and it will start executing it. During this stage, the browser displays a blank white screen, as the rest of the page is yet to be downloaded. Therefore, it is recommended to include the script at the bottom of the page, so that the browser will download all the HTML code and the user will have some content on the screen, while JavaScript is being downloaded in the background.

And that's it!

By this point, you should have a working installation of RaphaelJS and are free to play around and discover more about it.

Quick start – creating your first shape

Here, we will create the first shape in Raphael in two simple steps.

Step 1 – Creating a canvas to draw on

Initializing a Raphael object is as simple as munching a banana, and there are two ways to munch.

It can either be created directly in the browser's viewport (viewable area) or in an element. It's usually advisable to create the Raphael object in an element, probably a `Div` tag. It's important to keep in mind that the paper (drawing area) is the boundary of the x, y grid, not the browser's window.

Creating a canvas in the browser's viewport

The syntax for creating the Raphael object, which is the base for all other Raphael methods and functions, is as follows:

```
var raphaelObj = Raphael(x,y,width,height);
```

The four parameters inside the Raphael function are nothing but x-position, y-position, width, and height of the canvas to be created.

Since it is created in the browser's viewport, the positioning of the canvas will be absolute; therefore, it will overlap any HTML element underneath.

For example:

```
// Creating the canvas in the browser's viewport
var paper = Raphael(20, 30, 650, 400);
```

Downloading the example code

You can download the example code files for all Packt books you have purchased from your account at `http://www.PacktPub.com`. If you purchased this book elsewhere, you can visit `http://www.PacktPub.com/support` and register to have the files e-mailed directly to you.

Here the Raphael object is initialized and assigned to a variable called `paper`. This variable will be christened with all the powers of RaphaelJS. It will, henceforth, become the **Raphael Paper Object**.

Creating an object in an element (recommended)

To initiate the Raphael object inside an element, we must add the element ID or the element itself in the place of the positioning coordinates (x, y).

Let's consider the following example:

```
//The element itself is passed
//This line creates a Raphael paper inside 'paperDiv', which is 650px
in width and 400px in height
var elm= document.getElementById("paperDiv");
var paper = Raphael(elm, 650, 400);
//or
// The element ID is passed directly
//This line also creates a Raphael paper inside 'paperDiv', which is
650px in width and 400px in height
var paper = Raphael("paperDiv", 650, 400);
```

That's it; we now have the engine up and running.

Vrooom vrooom.

Step 2 – Drawing the circle

It is now time to shift gears.

The moment we assigned the Raphael object to the variable `paper`, it transforms itself into a magic wand, allowing us to pull off tricks to the best of our imagination.

There are certain predefined methods to create basic geometrical shapes such as circles, rectangles, and ellipses. Now we are going to spell out a circle with our shiny new wand.

A circle can be drawn using the `circle()` method. This method takes three parameters, namely x, y, and radius. Assign it to a variable that allows us to use it later in the code, specifically, to access the vector object easily for animations, transformations, and other effects.

The syntax is as follows:

```
var cir = paper.circle(x,y,r);
// x and y are the positioning co-ordinates, and "r" is the radius of
the circle
//Here the circle is assigned to a variable called cir.
//Example
var cir = paper.circle(35,25,20);
// This will create a circle of 20 pixels in radius at 35,25 (X & Y
axis).
```

The output for the preceding code is as shown in the following screenshot:

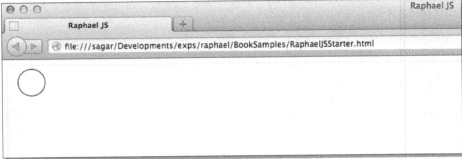

A circle created using RaphaelJS

The attr() method

We now have a smooth circle. It's absolutely fantastic, but wouldn't it be much better if we could add some color and other styles to it? RaphaelJS gives us the option to add styles to the object. It's a fairly straightforward method.

Styles and other customizations to our new circle are done using the `attr()` method.

This method takes the properties as parameters. The properties are entered as a collection of objects in key-value pairs. If you are familiar with jQuery, then its syntax is identical to jQuery's `attr()` method. This format is known as **JavaScript Object Notation (JSON)**, to further clarify.

The syntax for this method is as follows:

```
element.attr({
  "Property1":value1,
  "Property2":value2
})
```

Let's consider the following example:

```
//adding the attributes as key value pair
var coloredCircle = paper.circle(35,25,20).attr({
  "fill":"#17A9C6",
  "stroke":"#2A6570",
  "stroke-width":2
});
```

The output for the preceding code snippet is as shown in the following screenshot:

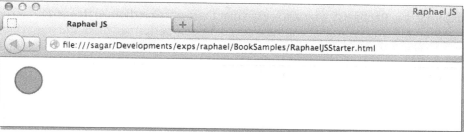

A circle with styles applied using the `attr()` method

Raphael's paper allows easy integration of vector graphics in an HTML layout, which makes it even more appealing.

Paper—the shiny new wand.

There are a ton of attributes available for each object and a list of all the objects can be found at the Raphael documentation. The URL can be found at the *People and places you should get to know* section, as an entire list of attributes is beyond the scope of this book.

Top features you need to know about

As you learn to use RaphaelJS, you will realize that there are a plethora of things you can do with it. This section will teach you all about the most commonly performed tasks and most commonly used features in RaphaelJS.

By the end of this section, you will be able to:

◆ Create a Raphael element

◆ Manipulate the style of the element

◆ Transform the element

◆ Perform animations on the element

◆ Add JavaScript events to the element

Creating a Raphael element

Creating a Raphael element is very easy. To make it better, there are predefined methods to create basic geometrical shapes.

Basic shape

There are three basic shapes in RaphaelJS, namely circle, ellipse, and rectangle. Since the circle is already covered in the *Quick start* section, we are going to skip drawing a circle.

Rectangle

We can create a rectangle using the `rect()` method. This method takes four required parameters and a fifth optional parameter, `border-radius`. The `border-radius` parameter will make the rectangle rounded (rounded corners) by the number of pixels specified.

The syntax for this method is:

```
paper.rect(X,Y,Width,Height,border-radius(optional));
```

A normal rectangle can be created using the following code snippet:

```
// creating a raphael paper in 'paperDiv'
var paper = Raphael ("paperDiv", 650,400);
// creating a rectangle with the rect() method. The four required
parameters are X,Y,Width & Height
var rect = paper.rect(35,25,170,100).attr({
  "fill":"#17A9C6", //filling with background color
  "stroke":"#2A6570", // border color of the rectangle
  "stroke-width":2 // the width of the border
});
```

The output for the preceding code snippet is shown in the following screenshot:

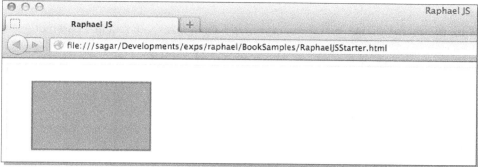

Plain rectangle

Rounded rectangle

The following code will create a basic rectangle with rounded corners:

```
// creating a raphael paper in 'paperDiv'
var paper = Raphael ("paperDiv", 650,400);
//The fifth parameter will make the rectangle rounded by the number of
pixels specified - A rectangle with rounded corners
var rect = paper.rect(35,25,170,100,20).attr({
  "fill":"#17A9C6",//background color of the rectangle
  "stroke":"#2A6570",//border color of the rectangle
  "stroke-width":2 // width of the border
});
//in the preceding code 20(highlighted) is the border-radius of the
rectangle.
```

The output for the preceding code snippet is a rectangle with rounded corners, as shown in the following screenshot:

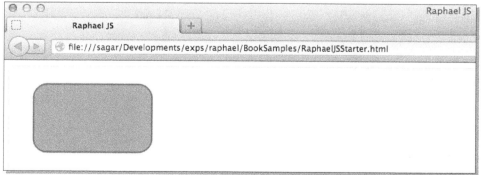

Rectangle with rounded corners

We can create other basic shapes in the same way. Let's create an ellipse with our magic wand.

Ellipse

An ellipse is created using the `ellipse()` method and it takes four required parameters, namely x,y, horizontal radius, and vertical radius. The horizontal radius will be the width of the ellipse divided by two and the vertical radius will be the height of the ellipse divided by two.

The syntax for creating an ellipse is:

```
paper.ellipse(X,Y,rX,rY);
//rX is the horizontal radius & rY is the vertical radius of the
ellipse
```

Let's consider the following example for creating an ellipse:

```
// creating a raphael paperin 'paperDiv'
var paper = Raphael ("paperDiv", 650,400);
//The ellipse() method takes four required parameters: X,Y, horizontal
radius & vertical Radius
var ellipse = paper.ellipse(195,125,170,100).attr({
  "fill":"#17A9C6", // background color of the ellipse
  "stroke":"#2A6570", // ellipse's border color
  "stroke-width":2 // border width
});
```

The preceding code will create an ellipse of width 170 x 2 and height 100 x 2.

An ellipse created using the `ellipse()` method is shown in the following screenshot:

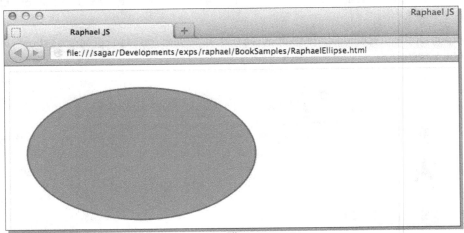

An Ellipse

Complex shapes

It's pretty easy to create basic shapes, but what about complex shapes such as stars, octagons, or any other shape which isn't a circle, rectangle, or an ellipse.

It's time for the next step of Raphael wizardry.

Complex shapes are created using the `path()` method which has only one parameter called `pathString`. Though the path string may look like a long genetic sequence with alphanumeric characters, it's actually very simple to read, understand, and draw with.

Before we get into path drawing, it's essential that we know how it's interpreted and the simple logic behind those complex shapes. Imagine that you are drawing on a piece of paper with a pencil. To draw something, you will place the pencil at a point in the paper and begin to draw a line or a curve and then move the pencil to another point on the paper and start drawing a line or curve again. After several such cycles, you will have a masterpiece—at least, you will call it a masterpiece.

Raphael uses a similar method to draw and it does so with a path string.

A typical path string may look like this: `M0,0L26,0L13,18L0,0`. Let's zoom into this path string a bit.

The first letter says `M` followed by `0,0`. That's right genius, you've guessed it correctly.

It says *move to* `0,0` position, the next letter `L` is *line to* `26,0`. RaphaelJS will move to `0,0` and from there draw a line to `26,0`. This is how the path string is understood by RaphaelJS and paths are drawn using these simple notations.

Here is a comprehensive list of commands and their respective meanings:

Command	Meaning expansion	Attributes
M	move to	(x, y)
Z	close path	(none)
L	line to	(x, y)
H	horizontal line to	x
V	vertical line to	y
C	curve to	(x1, y1, x2, y2, x, y)
S	smooth curve to	(x2, y2, x, y)
Q	quadratic Bézier curve to	(x1, y1, x, y)
T	smooth quadratic Bézier curve to	(x, y)
A	elliptical arc	(rx, ry, x axis-rotation, large-arc-flag, sweep-flag, x, y)
R	Catmull-Rom-curve to*	x1, y1 (x y)

The uppercase commands are absolute (M20, 20); they are calculated from the 0, 0 position of the drawing area (paper). The lowercase commands are relative (m20, 20); they are calculated from the last point where the pen left off.

There are so many commands, which might feel like too much to take in—don't worry; there is no need to remember every command and its format. Because we'll be using vector graphics editors to extract paths, it's essential that you understand the meaning of each and every command so that when someone asks you "hey genius, what does this mean?", you shouldn't be standing there clueless pretending to have not heard it.

The syntax for the `path()` method is as follows:

```
paper.path("pathString");
```

Let's consider the following example:

```
// creating a raphael paper in 'paperDiv'
var paper = Raphael ("paperDiv", 350,200);
// Creating a shape using the path() method and a path string
var tri = paper.path("M0,0L26,0L13,18L0,0").attr({
  "fill":"#17A9C6", // filling the background color
  "stroke":"#2A6570", // the color of the border
  "stroke-width":2 // the size of the border
});
```

 All these commands ("M0,0L26,0L13,18L0,0") use uppercase letters. They are therefore absolute values.

The output for the previous example is shown in the following screenshot:

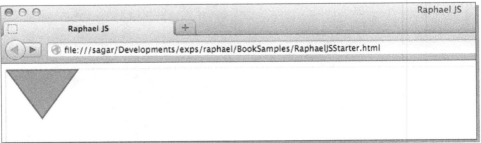

A triangle shape drawn using the path string

Extracting and using paths from an editor

Well, a triangle may be an easy shape to put into a path string. How about a complex shape such as a star? It's not that easy to guess and manually find the points. It's also impossible to create a fairly more complex shape like a simple flower or a 2D logo.

Here in this section, we'll see a simple but effective method of drawing complex shapes with minimal fuss and sharp accuracy.

Vector graphics editors

The vector graphics editors are meant for creating complex shapes with ease and they have some powerful tools in their disposal to help us draw. For this example, we'll create a star shape using an open source editor called Inkscape, and then extract those paths and use Raphael to get out the shape! It is as simple as it sounds, and it can be done in four simple steps.

Step 1 – Creating the shape in the vector editor

Let's create some star shapes in Inkscape using the built-in shapes tool.

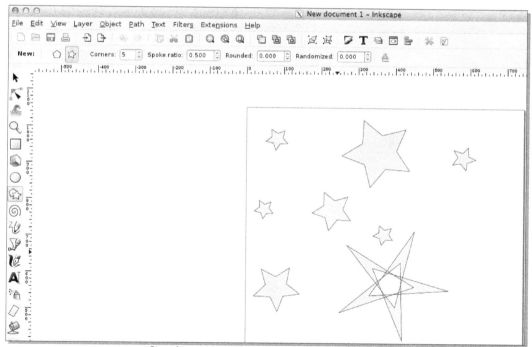

Star shapes created using the built-in shapes tool

Step 2 – Saving the shape as SVG

The paths used by SVG and RaphaelJS are similar. The trick is to use the paths generated by the vector graphics editor in RaphaelJS. For this purpose, the shape must be saved as an SVG file.

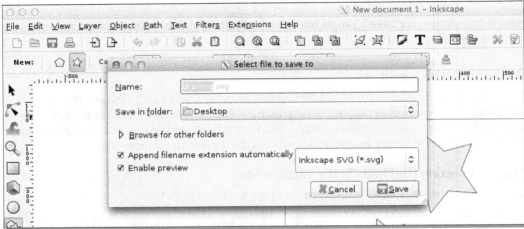

Saving the shape as an SVG file

Step 3 – Copying the SVG path string

The next step is to copy the path from SVG and paste it into Raphael's `path()` method.

SVG is a markup language, and therefore it's nested in tags. The SVG path can be found in the `<path>` and `</path>` tags. After locating the path tag, look for the `d` attribute. This will contain a long path sequence. You've now hit the bullseye.

```
50      <g
51          inkscape:label="Layer 1"
52          inkscape:groupmode="layer"
53  ▼       id="layer1">
54        <path
55          sodipodi:type="star"
56          style="fill:#ffff00;fill-rule:evenodd;stroke:#000000;stroke-width:1px;stroke-linecap:butt;stroke-linejoin:miter;stroke-opacit
57          id="path2985"
58          sodipodi:sides="5"
59          sodipodi:cx="232.85714"
60          sodipodi:cy="282.36218"
61          sodipodi:r1="55.640977"
62          sodipodi:r2="27.820489"
63          sodipodi:arg1="0.50959226"
64          sodipodi:arg2="1.1379108"
65          inkscape:flatsided="false"
66          inkscape:rounded="0"
67          inkscape:randomized="0"
68          d="m 281.42857,309.50504 -36.90095,-1.88856 -22.47547,29.32748 -9.6069,-35.67849 -34.83738,-12.31275 30.96356,-20.16197 0.944
69          inkscape:transform-center-x="3.3389269"
70          inkscape:transform-center-y="2.0365878" />
```

The path string is highlighted

Step 4 – Using the copied path as a Raphael path string

After copying the path string from SVG, paste it into Raphael's `path()` method.

```
var newpath=paper.path("copied path string from SVG").attr({
   "fill":"#5DDEF4",
   "stroke":"#2A6570",
   "stroke-width":2
});
```

That's it! We have created a complex shape in RaphaelJS with absolute simplicity.

 Using this technique, we can only extract the path, not the styles. So the background color, shadow, or any other style in the SVG won't apply. We need to add our own styles to the path objects using the `attr()` method.

A screenshot depicting the complex shapes created in RaphaelJS using the path string copied from an SVG file is shown here:

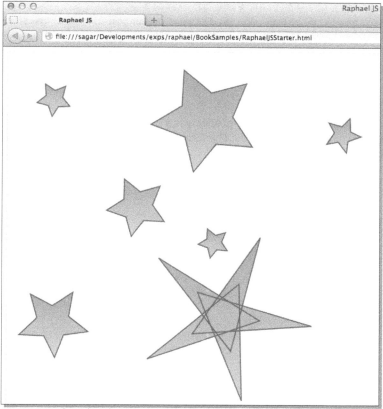

Complex shapes created in RaphaelJS using path string

Creating text

Text can be created using the `text()` method. Raphael gives us a way to add a battery of styles to the text object, right from changing colors to animating physical properties like position and size.

The `text()` method takes three required parameters, namely, x,y, and the text string.

The syntax for the `text()` method is as follows:

```
paper.text(X,Y,"Raphael JS Text");
// the text method with X,Y coordinates and the text string
```

Let's consider the following example:

```
// creating a raphael paper in 'paperDiv'
var paper = Raphael ("paperDiv", 650,400);
// creating text
var text = paper.text(40,55,"Raphael Text").attr({
  "fill":"#17A9C6", // font-color
  "font-size":75, // font size in pixels
//text-anchor indicates the starting position of the text relative to
the X, Y position.It can be "start", "middle" or  "end" default is
"middle"
"text-anchor":"start",
"font-family":"century gothic" // font family of the text
});
```

I am pretty sure that the `text-anchor` property is a bit heavy to munch. Well, there is a saying that a picture is worth a thousand words. The following diagram clearly explains the `text-anchor` property and its usage.

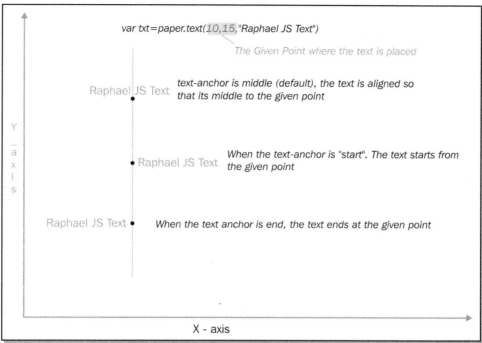

A brief explanation of text-anchor property

A screenshot of the text rendered using the text() method is as follows:

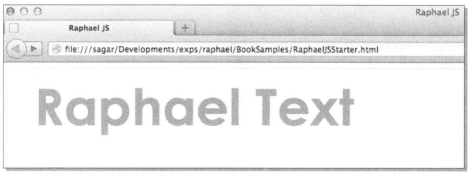

Rendering text using the text() method

Manipulating the style of the element

The `attr()` method not only adds styles to an element, but it also modifies an existing style of an element.

The following example explains the `attr()` method:

```
rect.attr('fill','#ddd');
// This will update the background color of the rectangle to gray
```

Transforming an element

RaphaelJS not only creates elements, but it also allows the manipulating or transforming of any element and its properties dynamically.

Manipulating a shape

By the end of this section, you would know how to transform a shape.

There might be many scenarios wherein you might need to modify a shape dynamically. For example, when the user mouse-overs a circle, you might want to scale up that circle just to give a visual feedback to the user. Shapes can be manipulated in RaphaelJS using the `transform()` method.

Transformation is done through the `transform()` method, and it is similar to the `path()` method where we add the path string to the method. `transform()` works in the same way, but instead of the path string, it's the transformation string. There is only a moderate difference between a transformation string and a path string.

There are four commands in the transformation string:

T	Translate
S	Scale
R	Rotate in degrees
M	Matrix

The fourth command, M, is of little importance and let's keep it out of the way, to avoid confusion.

> The transformation string might look similar to a path string. In reality, they are different, not entirely but significantly, sharing little in common. The M in a path string means *move to*, whereas the same in a transformation string means *Matrix*. The path string is not to be confused with a transformation string.

As with the path string, the uppercase letters are for absolute transformations and the lowercase for relative transformation. If the transformation string reads `r90T100,0`, then the element will rotate 90 degrees and move 100 px in the x axis (left). If the same reads `r90t100,0`, then the element will rotate 90 degrees and since the translation is relative, it will actually move vertically down 100px, as the rotation has tilted its axis.

I am sure the previous point will confuse most, so let me break it up.

Imagine a rectangle with a head and now this head is at the right side of the rectangle. For the time being, let's forget about absolute and relative transformation; our objective is to:

1. Rotate the rectangle by 90 degrees.
2. Move the rectangle 100px on the x axis (that is, 100px to the right).

It's critical to understand that the elements' original values don't change when we translate it, meaning its x and y values will remain the same, no matter how we rotate or move the element.

Now our first requirement is to rotate the rectangle by 90 degrees. The code for that would be `rect.transform("r90")` where `r` stands for rotation—fantastic, the rectangle is rotated by 90 degrees. Now pay attention to the next important step. We also need the rectangle to move 100px in the x axis and so we update our previous code to `rect.transform("r90t100,0")`, where `t` stands for translation. What happens next is interesting—the translation is done through a lowercase `t`, which means it's relative. One thing about relative translations is that they take into account any previous transformation applied to the element, whereas absolute translations simply reset any previous transformations before applying their own.

Remember the head of the rectangle on the right side? Well, the rectangle's x axis falls on the right side. So when we say, move 100px on the x axis, it is supposed to move 100px towards its right side, that is, in the direction where its head is pointing. Since we have rotated the rectangle by 90 degrees, its head is no longer on the right side but is facing the bottom.

So when we apply the relative translation, the rectangle will still move 100px to its x axis, but the x axis is now pointing down because of the rotation. That's why the rectangle will move 100px down when you expect it to move to the right.

What happens when we apply absolute translation is something that is entirely different from the previous one. When we again update our code for absolute translation to `rect.transform("r90T100,0")`, the axis of the rectangle is not taken into consideration. However, the axis of the paper is used, as absolute transformations don't take previous transformations into account, and they simply reset them before applying their own. Therefore, the rectangle will move 100px to the right after rotating 90 degrees, as intended.

 Absolute transformations will ignore all the previous transformations on that element, but relative transformations won't.

Getting a grip on this simple logic will save you a lot of frustration in the future while developing as well as while debugging.

The following is a screenshot depicting relative translation:

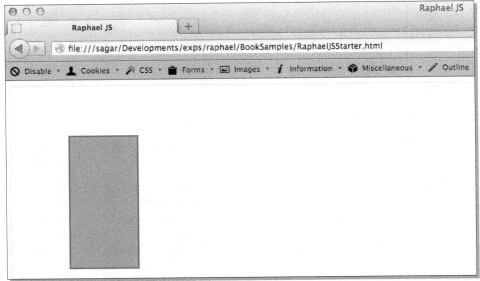

Using relative translation

The following is a screenshot depicting absolute translation:

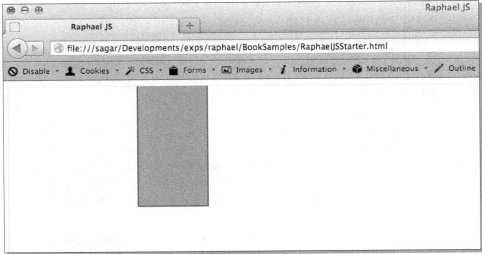

Using absolute translation

Notice the gap on top of the rotated rectangle; it's moved 100px on the one with relative translation and there is no such gap on top of the rectangle with absolute translation.

By default, the transform method will append to any transformation already applied to the element. To reset all transformations, use `element.transform("")`. Adding an empty string to the transform method will reset all the previous transformations on that element.

It's also important to note that the element's original x,y position will not change when translated. The element will merely assume a temporary position but its original position will remain unchanged. Therefore after translation, if we call for the element's position programmatically, we will get the original x,y, not the translated one, just so we don't jump from our seats and call RaphaelJS dull!

The following is an example of scaling and rotating a triangle:

```
//creating a Triangle using the path string
var tri = paper.path("M0,0L104,0L52,72L0,0").attr({
  "fill":"#17A9C6",
  "stroke":"#2A6570",
  "stroke-width":2
});
//transforming the triangle.
   tri.animate({
     "transform":"r90t100,0,s1.5"
   },1000);
//the transformation string should be read as rotating the element by
90 degrees, translating it to 100px in the X-axis and scaling up by
1.5 times
```

The following screenshot depicts the output of the preceding code:

Scaling and rotating a triangle

The triangle is transformed using relative translation (t). Now you know the reason why the triangle has moved down rather than moving to its right.

Animating a shape

What good is a magic wand if it can't animate inanimate objects! RaphaelJS can animate as smooth as butter almost any property from color, opacity, width, height, and so on with little fuss.

Animation is done through the `animate()` method. This method takes two required parameters, namely `final values` and `milliseconds`, and two optional parameters, `easing` and `callback`.

The syntax for the `animate()` method is as follows:

```
Element.animate({
    Animation properties in key value pairs
},time,easing,callback_function);
```

Easing is that special effect with which the animation is done, for example, if the easing is bounce, the animation will appear like a bouncing ball. The following are the several easing options available in RaphaelJS:

- `linear`
- `<` or `easeIn` or `ease-in`
- `>` or `easeOut` or `ease-out`
- `<>` or `easeInOut` or `ease-in-out`
- `backIn` or `back-in`
- `backOut` or `back-out`
- `elastic`
- `bounce`

Callbacks are functions that will execute when the animation is complete, allowing us to perform some tasks after the animation.

Let's consider the example of animating the width and height of a rectangle:

```
// creating a raphael paper in 'paperDiv'
var paper = Raphael ("paperDiv", 650,400);
rect.animate({
   "width":200, // final width
   "height":200 // final height
},300,'bounce',function(){
   // something to do when the animation is complete - this callback
function is optional
```

```
// Print 'Animation complete' when the animation is complete
$("#animation_status").html("Animation complete")
})
```

The following screenshot shows a rectangle before animation:

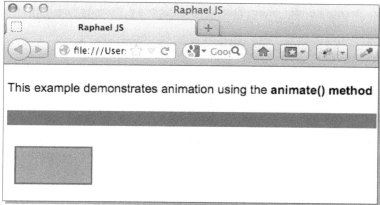

Rectangle before animation

A screenshot demonstrating the use of a callback function when the animation is complete is as follows. The text **Animation complete** will appear in the browser after completing the animation.

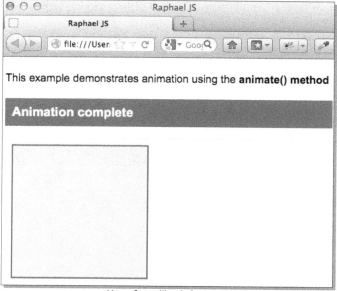

Use of a callback function

The following code animates the background color and opacity of a rectangle:

```
rect.animate({
  "fill":"#ddd", // final color,
  "fill-opacity":0.7
},300,"easeIn",function(){
  // something to do when the animation is complete - this call back
function is optional
  // Alerts done when the animation is complete
  alert("done");
})
```

Here the rectangle is animated from blue to gray and with an opacity from 1 to 0.7 over a duration of 300 milliseconds.

 Opacity in RaphaelJS is the same as in CSS, where 1 is opaque and 0 is transparent.

Animating transformations

The transformations can be animated using the transformation string.

Let's consider the following example:

```
//animating the rotation and scaling of a rectangle
rect.animate({
// animating with a rotation of 45 degree and scaling up 1.5 times
transform:"r45s1.5"
},500)
```

The following is a screenshot of a rectangle before animation:

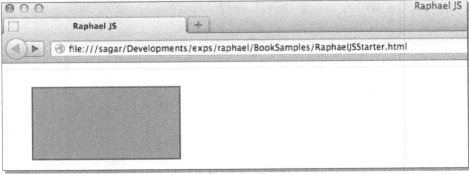

Before animation

The following is a screenshot of the same rectangle after animation:

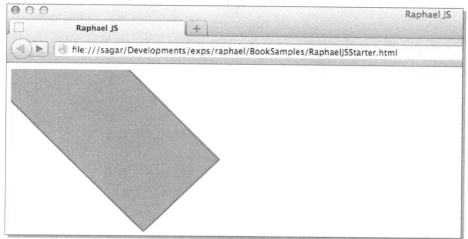

After animation

Animation can be done on almost any property.

Animation is an awesome feature and it's really smooth. But it comes at a cost; it takes up precious browser resources. It won't drain the browser leaving it out of juice, but reckless use of animation will have a significant impact on the end performance. Therefore, the developer must use animations wisely, so that it adds value to the entire user experience rather than annoying the user.

Adding events to Raphael elements

Adding events to elements is like injecting life into them. They take the drawings to the next level. Events can be added to elements using the various event handlers. In fact, all the normal JavaScript events are available for any Raphael element.

Here is an example of `click` and `mouseover` events.

Click event

The mouse click event can be added using the `click()` method.

Let's consider the following example:

```
//creating a raphael paper in 'paperDiv'
var paper = Raphael("paperDiv", 650, 400);
var blueStyle={
```

```
    "fill":"#5DDEF4",
    "stroke":"#2A6570",
    "stroke-width":2
}
//creating a plain circle
var cir = paper.circle(120,120,30).attr(blueStyle);
cir.click(function(){
  alert('Clicked circle');
})
```

The following is a screenshot demonstrating the click event handler:

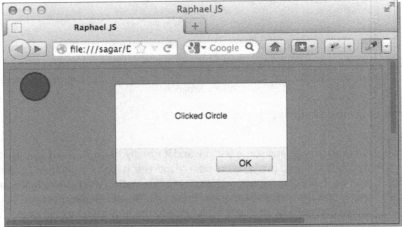

Click event handler

Mouseover event

The mouseover event can be added using the mouseover() method.

The following is an example of the mouseover() method:

```
// creating a circle with blue background
var cir = paper.circle(35,25,20).attr({
  "fill":"#17A9C6",
  "stroke":"#2A6570",
  "stroke-width":2
});
// adding mouseover event to the circle with the mouseover() event
handler
cir.mouseover(function(){
cir.animate({
  "fill":"#15EA18",
  "transform":"s2"
```

```
   },400)
 })
 // The preceding code animates the background color and scales up the
 circle twice on mouseover
```

Methods you'll want to know and use

This section will cover only the most common and frequent methods, as an entire list of attributes and methods is beyond the scope of this book.

Element methods

These methods can only be used with an element and not directly. For example, `rect.click()`.

animate()

The `animate()` method is used to animate various properties of the element for a specified duration.

The syntax for this method is as follows:

```
element.animate({
   Property1:value,
   Property2:value
},time_in_milliseconds,easing(optional),
callback_function(optional));
```

The following is an example of the `animate()` method:

```
rect.animate({
   "width":"300",
   "height":"200"
},500,'bounce',function(){
//something to do after animation
   alert("animation complete")
})
```

attr()

The `attr()` method is a very important method that is used to add attributes such as styles and other physical properties such as position, height, width, and so on to the element. It takes values in key value pairs.

The syntax for this method is as follows:

```
element.attr({
   Property1:value,
   Property2:value
})
```

The following is an example of the `attr()` method:

```
// Adding background color and stroke to a rectangle
rect.attr({
    "fill":"#17A9C6",    // Adds a background color
    "stroke":"#2A6570",  // the color of the border
    "stroke-width":2     // the width of the border
})
```

click()

The `click()` method is used to bind the `click` event to Raphael elements.

The following is an example of the `click()` method:

```
rect.click(function(){
    //something to do when the rectangle is clicked
    alert("clicked rectangle");
})
```

dblclick()

The `dblclick()` method adds the `double click` event to the element.

The following is an example of the `dblclick()` method:

```
cir.dblclick(function(){
    //alerts "it's a double click " when double clicked
    alert("It's a double click !");
})
```

mousedown()

The `mousedown()` method binds the `mousedown` event to Raphael elements—it triggers when any mouse button is pressed down.

The following is an example of the `mousedown()` method:

```
rect.mousedown(function(){
// The rectangle will animate to 200px wide when any mouse button is
pressed down
rect.animate({
    'width':'200'
    },400)
})
```

mouseup()

The `mouseup()` event binds the `mouseup` event to Raphael elements—it triggers when any mouse button is released.

The following is an example of the `mouseup()` method:

```
rect.mouseup(function(){
// The rectangle will animate to 100px wide any mouse button is
released
rect.animate({
  'width':'100'
  },400)
})
```

mousemove()

The `mousemove()` method triggers when the mouse is moved over the element.

The following is an example of the `mousemove()` method:

```
// increases the size of the rectangle as the mouse moves over the
rectangle.
var wd=100 // Intial width
rect.mousemove(function(){
  wd++ // incrementing the width on mouse move
  rect.attr({
    //setting the width of the rectangle with the attr() method
    'width':wd
  });
})
```

mouseover()

The `mouseover()` method triggers when the mouse enters the Raphael element.

The following is an example of the `mouseover()` method:

```
//animating the size of the circle when the mouse enters the circle
cir.mouseover(function(){
  cir.animate({
  transform:'s2' // scaling up the circle twice
  },500,'elastic'); //adding and elastic easing function to the
animation
})
```

mouseout()

The mouseout() method triggers when the mouse leaves the Raphael element.

The following is an example of the mouseout() method:

```
// scaling down the size of the circle when the mouse leaves it
cir.mouseout(function(){
  cir.animate({
    transform:'s0.5' // scaling down the circle to half of its original
size
  },500,'bounce') //adding and elastic easing function to the
animation
})
```

clone()

There will be situations where we will want to duplicate an element. Some might say, "Ah ! that's easy, I just need to copy the element to a new variable like var newrect=rect". Well, it looks like you have made a copy, but that won't work for sure. The variable acts as a reference to the object, in this case, the rectangle. So when we copy the variable, we are just copying the reference. In reality, the new variable still points to the same old object. Here is an example of the wrong way:

```
// assigning the rect to a new variable called newRect
var newRect=rect;
newRect.attr({
  fill:'#ddd',
  transform:'t100,100'
})
```

The following screenshot demonstrates what happens when the variable is duplicated—there is no clone of the rectangle.

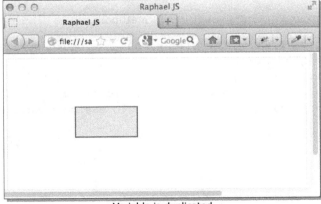

Variable is duplicated

It's obvious that copying the variable didn't work, as it's evident that the background color has been applied to the same rectangle, and there is no second rectangle as there is supposed to be.

This problem can be addressed by the `clone()` method in a simple and elegant way.

```
//To duplicate a rectangle
var newRect=rect.clone();
newRect.attr({
  fill:'#ddd',
  transform:'t100,100'
})
```

Using the `clone()` method instead of duplicating the variable will produce a clone of the rectangle, as depicted in the following screenshot:

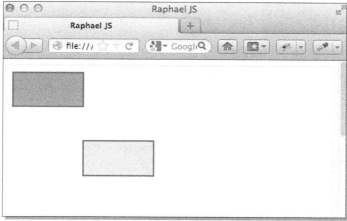

Producing a clone using the clone() method

Now, we see two rectangles and the background color of the second rectangle is now gray as intended.

data()

Raphael has an incredibly simple way to assign some data to each and every element and retrieve it on demand. It's as simple as assigning some data to an element while creating it and recalling that data whenever necessary. It's a simple and straightforward way.

Data can be added to an element using the `data()` method in key value pairs.

The following is an example of the `data()` method:

```
//assigning a name to a circle
cir.data('name','Am Raphael JS');
// retrieving the data
```

```
cir.click(function(){
  alert(this.data('name'));
})
```

The following is a screenshot depicting the data contents of the circle when clicked:

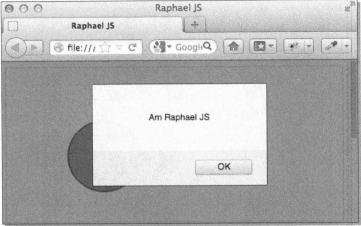

Data contents of the circle when clicked

removedata()

The removedata() method takes the key as a parameter. If the key isn't provided, it will remove all the associated data.

The syntax for this method is:

```
removedata(key)
```

The following is an example of the removedata() method:

```
//removing the name of the circle
cir.removeData('name') // removes the name of the circle
```

getBBox()

The getBBox() method returns the bounding box of the element. By default, the bounding will take into account any transformations on the element. To get the bounding box before any transformation is applied on the element, the isWithoutTransform parameter must be set to true.

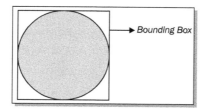

The following is an example of the getBBox() method:

```
cir.getBBox() // returns the bounding box
cir.getBBox({
isWithoutTransform:true // this will return the bouding box values
before any transformation that has been applied on the element. It
will still return the old values ignoring the transformations
})
```

The getBBox() method returns an object with the following values:

Value	Type	Description
X	Number	Top-left corner's x position
Y	Number	Top-left corner's y position
X2	Number	Bottom-right corner's x position
Y2	Number	Bottom-right corner's y position
Width	Number	Width of the bounding box
Height	Number	Height of the bounding box

getPointAtLength()

The getPointAtLength() method returns the coordinates of the point at a particular length of a path. The getPointAtLength() method takes two parameters, namely path and length.

The syntax for this method is:

```
getPointAtLength(path,length)
```

The path must be a path string and the length a number.

The getPointAtLength() method returns an object with the following values:

Value	Type	Description
X	Number	The x coordinate of the point
Y	Number	The y coordinate of the point
Alpha	Number	The angle of the derivative

toFront()

The `toFront()` method brings the element to the forefront on top of all other elements. Its function is similar to **CSS z-index**. It doesn't take any parameters.

The following is an example of the `toFront()` method:

```
cir.toFront();//brings the circle on top of all the elements
```

The following screenshot demonstrates the use of the `toFront()` method. The circle is brought to the front by using the `toFront()` method; therefore, it overlaps the rectangle.

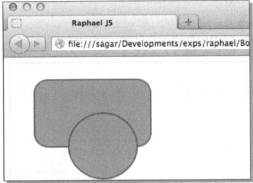

Circle brought to the front using the toFront() method

toBack()

The `toBack()` method is the exact opposite of the `toFront()` method, as it moves the element behind all the other elements.

The following is an example of the `toBack()` method:

```
rect.toBack() // moves the rect behind all the elements
```

hide()

The `hide()` method makes the element invisible. This method is the Raphael equivalent of `visibility:hidden` or `display:none` in CSS.

The following is an example of the `hide()` method:

```
rect.hide()
```

show()

The `show()` method makes the element visible.

The following is an example of the `show()` method:

```
rect.show()
```

transform()

The `transform()` method adds a transformation to a given element. It takes only one parameter and it's the transformation string.

The syntax for this method is as follows:

```
transform([transformationString]);
```

The following is an example of the `transform()` method:

```
rect.transform("s1.5t100,100,r90");
//scales the rectangle to 1.5 times larger and then translates it to
100px in the X-axis, 100px in the Y-axis and finally rotating it by 90
degrees
//Transformation can also be done using the attr() method.
element.attr('transform','s1.5t100,100,r90');
```

remove()

The `remove()` method removes the element from the paper.

The following is an example of the `remove()` method:

```
rect.remove();
//the preceding line removes the rect from Raphael paper
```

Paper methods

The paper methods can only be used with the Raphael paper object.

paper.circle()

The `paper.circle()` method creates a circle.

The following is the syntax for this method:

```
circle(x,y,radius);
```

Where x is the x position of the circle, y is the y position of the circle, and `radius` is the radius of the circle.

The following is an example of the `paper.circle()` method:

```
var cir=paper.circle(100,50,20);
```

paper.ellipse()

The `paper.ellipse()` method creates an ellipse.

The following is the syntax for this method:

```
ellipse(x,y,rx,ry);
```

where x is the x position of the circle, y is the y position of the circle, rx is the horizontal radius, and ry is the vertical radius.

The following is an example of the `paper.ellipse()` method:

```
var ell = paper.ellipse(15,30,80,50);
```

paper.rect()

The `paper.rect()` method creates a simple rectangle.

The following is a syntax for this method:

```
rect(x,y,width,height,radius(optional));
```

Where x is the x position of the circle, y is the y position of the circle, width is the width of the rectangle, and height is the height of the rectangle. It also has a last fifth parameter — the border radius of the rectangle, which will add a curved edge of the given radius to the rectangle. Rounded corners do look smooth. Though the method's name is rect(), it can be used to create a box of any shape. It is not restricted to create perfect rectangles.

The following is an example of the `paper.rect()` method:

```
// A rectangle with a border radius of 5px
var rectangle = paper.rect(10,10,50,70,5);
```

paper.clear()

The `paper.clear()` method is used to clear the drawing canvas. This is the magical broom. The `paper.clear()` method doesn't take any parameters; it wipes it all.

The following is an example of the `paper.clear()` method:

```
paper.clear()
```

paper.image()

Raphael is good at drawing, and using Raphael we can replace some images with it. But that doesn't mean it's an image replacement solution; Raphael can only substitute. It's, therefore, wrong to consider it as a complete replacement for images. However, images can be manipulated in Raphael.

The `paper.image()` method allows us to import images on to the paper. This method takes the following five parameters:

Parameter	Description
src	The path of the image
X	The x coordinate point where the image should be placed
Y	The y coordinate point where the image should be placed
Width	The width of the image
Height	The height of the image

The following is an example of the `paper.image()` method:

```
var img=paper.image("images/world.png",10,15,80,100);
//imports an image called world.png and places it at 10,15 position.
Sets the image's width to 80px and height to 100px
```

And now the imported image is converted into a Raphael object. All the usual transformations can be applied to that image object.

paper.setSize()

The `paper.setSize()` method is a very handy method. This method allows the resizing of the Raphael paper object, so that you don't run out of space. This method takes two required parameters, namely, width and height—these will be the new width and height of the Raphael paper.

The following is the syntax of this method:

```
paper.setSize(width,height);
```

The following is an example of the `paper.setSize()` method:

```
paper.setSize(500,600);
//500 and 600 will be the new width and height of the paper.
```

paper.set()

The `paper.set()` method groups several Raphael objects, and any action performed on this set will apply to all the elements. The `set()` method merely groups the elements, it doesn't create any copies of the elements. Deleting a set will have no effect on the elements.

It is worth mentioning that sets in RaphaelJS are ordered. This varies from the set type in Python, which is a group of unordered objects.

The following is the syntax for this method:

```
var raphaelSet=paper.set();
raphaelSet.push(element1,element2, ...);
```

The following is an example of the `paper.set()` method:

```
// the following code will create a new set called raphaelSet, add
elements to it and change the color of the set to red
var raphaelSet=paper.set();//creating a new set
// adding elements to the set using the push() method
raphaelSet.push(circle,rect,ellipse);
//changing the color of the set - this will affect all the elements in
the set.
raphaelSet.attr('fill','red');
```

The following is a screenshot demonstrating the use of the `paperset()` method in RaphaelJS.

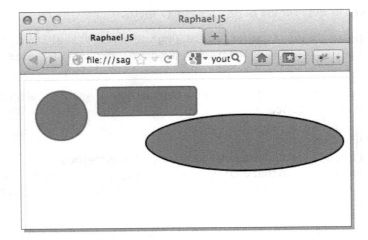

Changing the color of the set to red changes the color of all the elements in the set.

Set methods

The set methods can only be used with the set object, created using the `set()` method.

```
var raphaelSet=paper.set();
//raphaelSet is now a set object to which all the set methods apply.
```

set.clear()

The `set.clear()` method removes all the elements from the set. The `set()` method only groups elements together, it doesn't duplicate any elements. Therefore, when a set is cleared, no elements are removed, they are just unbounded.

The following is the syntax of this method:

```
Set.clear();
```

The following is an example of the `set.clear()` method:

```
raphaelSet.clear();
// The preceding code will remove the set called raphaelSet, not its
elements
```

set.exclude()

Clearing a set seems to be simple—a call to the clear method and kaboom, everything is gone. What about precision picking? RaphaelJS provides the `set.exclude()` method, which can be used to remove only a particular element from the set. This method takes only one required parameter, that is, the element to be removed. Want to remove a black sheep? No problem.

The following is the syntax of this method:

```
set.exclude(element);
```

The following is an example of the `set.exclude()` method:

```
raphaelSet.exclude(rect);
//The preceding code removes the element called 'rect' from the set
'raphaelSet'
```

set.forEach()

The `set.forEach()` method executes a function for every element of the set. The callback function takes only one parameter, which is a reference to the current element in the loop.

The following is the syntax of this method:

```
set.forEach(callback_function,thisArg);
```

The following is an example of the `set.forEach()` method:

```
raphaelSet.forEach(function(elm){
  elm.attr('fill','green');
})
// The preceding code will loop through all the elements in the
raphaelSet and change the background color of each and every element
to green.
```

set.pop()

The `set.pop()` method removes the last element from the set and returns it.

The following is an example of the `set.pop()` method:

```
raphaelSet.pop();
// the preceding code will remove the last element from the raphaelSet
and return the removed element.
```

set.splice()

The set.splice() method is used to delete and insert an element. This method takes three parameters, namely, index, count, and element, which are to be inserted. Index is where the element should be deleted, count is the number of elements to remove from the index position, and finally, the element to be inserted.

The following is the syntax of this method:

```
set.splice(index, count, element);
```

The following is an example of the set.splice() method:

```
var rect=paper.rect(10,10,50,100).attr('fill','green');
raphaelSet.splice(1,2,rect);
// The preceding code will remove two elements from the index position
of 1 and add a rect element.
```

People and places you should get to know

If you need help with RaphaelJS, here are some people and places that will prove invaluable.

Official sites

The official sites for all the official information regarding RaphaelJS are:

+ **Homepage**: http://raphaeljs.com/
+ **Manual and documentation**: http://raphaeljs.com/reference.html
+ **Twitter**: http://twitter.com/RaphaelJS/
+ **Source code**: https://github.com/DmitryBaranovskiy/raphael/

Articles and tutorials

A useful list of articles and tutorials for further reference and reading is as follows:

+ http://www.alistapart.com/articles/using-svg-for-flexible-scalable-and-fun-backgrounds-part-i
+ http://www.alistapart.com/articles/cross-platform-scalable-vector-graphics-with-svgweb/
+ http://net.tutsplus.com/tutorials/javascript-ajax/an-introduction-to-the-raphael-js-library/: An introduction to the RaphaelJS Library, from net tuts+
+ http://www.w3.org/TR/SVG11/: W3C SVG specification
+ http://www.irunmywebsite.com/raphael/additionalhelp.php#pagetop: An exhaustive list of RaphaelJS examples
+ http://inkscape.org/download/: A link for downloading Inkscape

Community

Official RaphaelJS communities and forums:

+ **Official forums**: https://groups.google.com/forum/?fromgroups#!forum/raphaeljs
+ **User FAQ**: http://raphaeljs.com/

Blogs

Official RaphaelJS blog:

◆ The blog of Dmitry Baranovskiy, the creator of RaphaelJS and various other libraries: `http://dmitry.baranovskiy.com/`

Twitter

RaphaelJS tweets:

◆ Follow RaphaelJS on Twitter at `http://twitter.com/RaphaelJS/`

◆ For more open source information, follow Packt at `http://twitter.com/#!/packtopensource`

Summary

RaphaelJS is a versatile and easy-to-use vector graphics library, allowing us to do tasks which were unthinkable a few years ago. Though HTML5 Canvas was inspired from vector graphics, it doesn't mean that it's a replacement for SVG, rather they compliment each other. Today's browsers have faster and better JavaScript engines that make rendering vector graphics even better.

From a user perspective, adding a little interactivity will make the site more interesting and engaging, and for this, vector graphics libraries like RaphaelJS are key. They make applications stand apart from the standard boxes and lines. RaphaelJS does add glitter to our applications and makes us completely rethink how we present our data. RaphaelJS is more versatile in the hands of the most creative, and that's what this book is all about—realizing the creative potential of RaphaelJS.

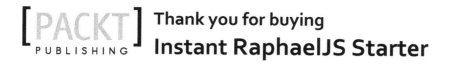

About Packt Publishing

Packt, pronounced 'packed', published its first book "*Mastering phpMyAdmin for Effective MySQL Management*" in April 2004 and subsequently continued to specialize in publishing highly focused books on specific technologies and solutions.

Our books and publications share the experiences of your fellow IT professionals in adapting and customizing today's systems, applications, and frameworks. Our solution based books give you the knowledge and power to customize the software and technologies you're using to get the job done. Packt books are more specific and less general than the IT books you have seen in the past. Our unique business model allows us to bring you more focused information, giving you more of what you need to know, and less of what you don't.

Packt is a modern, yet unique publishing company, which focuses on producing quality, cutting-edge books for communities of developers, administrators, and newbies alike. For more information, please visit our website: www.packtpub.com.

Writing for Packt

We welcome all inquiries from people who are interested in authoring. Book proposals should be sent to author@packtpub.com. If your book idea is still at an early stage and you would like to discuss it first before writing a formal book proposal, contact us; one of our commissioning editors will get in touch with you.

We're not just looking for published authors; if you have strong technical skills but no writing experience, our experienced editors can help you develop a writing career, or simply get some additional reward for your expertise.

jQuery Mobile Cookbook

ISBN: 978-1-84951-722-5   Paperback: 320 pages

Over 80 recipes with examples and practical tips to help you quickly learn and develop cross-platform applications with jQuery Mobile

1. Create applications that use custom animations and use various techniques to improve application performance

2. Use and customize the various controls such as toolbars, buttons, and lists with custom icons, icon sprites, styles, and themes

3. Write simple but powerful scripts to manipulate the various configurations and work with the events, methods, and utilities which are provided by the framework

Ext JS 4 Web Application Development Cookbook

ISBN: 978-1-84951-686-0   Paperback: 488 pages

Over 110 easy-to-follow recipes backed up with real-life examples, walking you through basic Ext JS features to advanced application design using Sencha's Ext JS

1. Learn how to build Rich Internet Applications with the latest version of the Ext JS framework in a cookbook style

2. From creating forms to theming your interface, you will learn the building blocks for developing the perfect web application

3. Easy to follow recipes step through practical and detailed examples which are all fully backed up with code, illustrations, and tips

Please check www.PacktPub.com for information on our titles

HTML5 Games Development by Example: Beginner's Guide

ISBN: 978-1-84969-126-0   Paperback: 352 pages

Create six fun games using the latest HTML5, Canvas, CSS, and JavaScript techniques

1. Learn HTML5 game development by building six fun example projects

2. Full, clear explanations of all the essential techniques

3. Covers puzzle games, action games, multiplayer, and Box 2D physics

4. Use the Canvas with multiple layers and sprite sheets for rich graphical games

Getting Started with Meteor.js JavaScript Framework

ISBN: 978-1-78216-082-3   Paperback: 130 pages

Develop modern web applications in Meteor, one of the hottest new JavaScript platforms

1. Create dynamic, multi-user web applications completely in JavaScript

2. Use best practice design patterns including MVC, templates, and data synchronization

3. Create simple, effective user authentication including Facebook and Twitter integration

4. Learn the time-saving techniques of Meteor to code powerful, lightning-fast web apps in minutes

Please check www.PacktPub.com for information on our titles